Everything Men Know About Women

Everything Men Know About Women

Everything Men Know About Women

Everything Men Know About Women

Everything Men Know About Women

Printed in Great Britain
by Amazon

34738332R00059